MW01610038

Cowboysology Trivia Challenge

Dallas Cowboys Football

Cowboysology Trivia Challenge

Dallas Cowboys Football

Researched by Billy G. Wilcox III

Paul F. Wilson & Tom P. Rippey III, Editors

Kick The Ball, Ltd

Lewis Center, Ohio

Trivia by Kick The Ball, Ltd

College Football Trivia

Alabama Crimson Tide	Auburn Tigers	Boston College Eagles	Florida Gators
Georgia Bulldogs	LSU Tigers	Miami Hurricanes	Michigan Wolverines
Nebraska Cornhuskers	Notre Dame Fighting Irish	Ohio State Buckeyes	Oklahoma Sooners
Oregon Ducks	Penn State Nittany Lions	Southern Cal Trojans	Texas Longhorns

Pro Football Trivia

Arizona Cardinals	Baltimore Ravens	Buffalo Bills	Chicago Bears
Cleveland Browns	Dallas Cowboys	Denver Broncos	Green Bay Packers
Indianapolis Colts	Kansas City Chiefs	Minnesota Vikings	New England Patriots
New Orleans Saints	New York Giants	New York Jets	Oakland Raiders
Philadelphia Eagles	Pittsburgh Steelers	San Francisco 49ers	Washington Redskins

Pro Baseball Trivia

Atlanta Braves	Baltimore Orioles	Boston Red Sox	Chicago Cubs
Chicago White Sox	Cincinnati Reds	Detroit Tigers	Houston Astros
Los Angeles Dodgers	Milwaukee Brewers	Minnesota Twins	New York Mets
New York Yankees	Philadelphia Phillies	Saint Louis Cardinals	San Francisco Giants

College Basketball Trivia

Duke Blue Devils	Georgetown Hoyas	Indiana Hoosiers	Kansas Jayhawks
Kentucky Wildcats	Maryland Terrapins	Michigan State Spartans	North Carolina Tar Heels
Syracuse Orange	UConn Huskies	UCLA Bruins	

Pro Basketball Trivia

Boston Celtics	Chicago Bulls	Detroit Pistons	Los Angeles Lakers
Utah Jazz			

Visit **www.TriviaGameBooks.com** for more details.

This book is dedicated to our families and friends for your unwavering love, support, and your understanding of our pursuit of our passions. Thank you for everything you do for us and for making our lives complete.

**Cowboysology Trivia Challenge: Dallas Cowboys Football;
First Edition 2011**

Published by
Kick The Ball, Ltd
8595 Columbus Pike, Suite 197
Lewis Center, OH 43035
www.TriviaGameBooks.com

Edited by: Paul F. Wilson & Tom P. Rippey III
Copy Edited by: Ashley Thomas Memory
Designed and Formatted by: Paul F. Wilson
Researched by: Billy G. Wilcox III

Copyright © 2011 by Kick The Ball, Ltd, Lewis Center, Ohio

ALL RIGHTS RESERVED. No part of this book may be reproduced or transmitted in any form whatsoever, electronic, or mechanical, including photocopying, recording, or by any informational storage or retrieval system without the expressed written, dated and signed permission from the copyright holder.

Trademarks and Copyrights: Kick The Ball, Ltd is not associated with any event, team, conference, or league mentioned in this book. All trademarks are the property of their respective owners. Kick The Ball, Ltd respects and honors the copyrights and trademarks of others. We use event, team, conference, or league names only as points of reference in titles, questions, answers, and other sections of our trivia game books. Names, statistics, and others facts obtained through public domain resources.

LIMIT OF LIABILITY/DISCLAIMER OF WARRANTY: THE RESEARCHER AND PUBLISHER HAVE USED GREAT CARE IN RESEARCHING AND WRITING THIS BOOK. HOWEVER, WE MAKE NO REPRESENTATION OR WARRANTIES AS TO THE COMPLETENESS OF ITS CONTENTS OR THEIR ACCURACY AND WE SPECIFICALLY DISCLAIM ANY IMPLIED WARRANTIES OF MERCHANTABILITY OR FITNESS FOR A PARTICULAR PURPOSE. WARRANTIES MAY NOT BE CREATED OR EXTENDED BY ANY SALES MATERIALS OR SALESPERSON OF THIS BOOK. NEITHER THE RESEARCHER NOR THE PUBLISHER SHALL BE LIABLE FOR ANY LOSS OF PROFIT OR ANY OTHER COMMERCIAL DAMAGES, INCLUDING BUT NOT LIMITED TO SPECIAL, INCIDENTAL, CONSEQUENTIAL, OR OTHER DAMAGES.

For information on ordering this book in bulk at reduced prices, please email us at pfwilson@triviagamebooks.com.

International Standard Book Number: 978-1-613320-007-0
Printed and Bound in the United States of America
10 9 8 7 6 5 4 3 2 1

Table of Contents

Dear Friend,

Thank you for purchasing our **Cowboysology Trivia Challenge** game book!

We have made every attempt to verify the accuracy of the questions and answers contained in this book. However it is still possible that from time to time an error has been made by us or our researchers. In the event you find a question or answer that is questionable or inaccurate, we ask for your understanding and thank you for bringing it to our attention so we may improve future editions of this book. Please email us at tprippey@triviagamebooks.com with those observations and comments.

Have fun playing **Cowboysology Trivia Challenge**!

Paul & Tom

Paul Wilson and Tom Rippey
Co-Founders, Kick The Ball, Ltd

PS – You can discover more about all of our current trivia game books by visiting www.TriviaGameBooks.com.

How to Play

Book Format:

There are four quarters, each made up of fifty questions. Each quarter's questions have assigned point values. Questions are designed to get progressively more difficult as you proceed through each quarter, as well as through the book itself. Most questions are in a four-option multiple-choice format so that you will at least have a 25% chance of getting a correct answer for some of the more challenging questions.

We have even added Overtime in the event of a tie, or just in case you want to keep playing a little longer.

Game Options:

One Player -
To play on your own, simply answer each of the questions in all the quarters, and in the overtime section, if you'd like. Use the Player / Team Score Sheet to record your answers and the quarter Answer Keys to check your answers. Calculate each quarter's points and the total for the game at the bottom of the Player / Team Score Sheet to determine your final score.

Two or More Players –
To play with multiple players decide if you will all be competing with each other individually, or if you will form and play as teams. Each player / team will then have its own Player / Team Score Sheet to record its answer. You can use the quarter Answer Keys to check your answers and to calculate your final scores.

The Player / Team Score Sheets have been designed so that each team can answer all questions or you can divide the questions up in any combination you would prefer. For example, you may want to alternate questions if two players are playing or answer every third question for three players, etc. In any case, simply record your response to your questions in the corresponding quarter and question number on the Player / Team Score Sheet.

A winner will be determined by multiplying the total number of correct answers for each quarter by the point value per quarter, then adding together the final total for all quarters combined. Play the game again and again by alternating the questions that your team is assigned so that you will answer a different set of questions each time you play.

You Create the Game -
There are countless other ways of using *Cowboysology Trivia Challenge* questions. It is limited only to your imagination. Examples might be using them at your tailgate or other professional football related party. Players / Teams who answer questions incorrectly may have to perform a required action, or winners may receive special prizes. Let us know what other games you come up with!

Have fun!

1) What year did the Cowboys play their first-ever game?

Answers begin on page 17

    A)   1956
    B)   1958
    C)   1960
    D)   1962

2) What is the name of the official mascot for the Dallas Cowboys?

    A)   Roscoe
    B)   Rocky
    C)   Randy
    D)   Rowdy

3) What year did Cowboys Stadium open?

    A)   2007
    B)   2008
    C)   2009
    D)   2010

4) Who holds the Cowboys franchise record for most career games played?

    A)   Ed Jones
    B)   Rayfield Wright
    C)   Bill Bates
    D)   Bob Lilly

5) Jon Kitna had a better completion percentage than Tony Romo during the Cowboys' 2010 regular season.

    A) True
    B) False

6) In which NFL Division does Dallas play?

    A) NFC East
    B) NFC South
    C) NFC West
    D) NFC North

7) Where did Dallas quarterback Tony Romo play college football?

    A) Wisconsin
    B) Western Michigan
    C) Northern Iowa
    D) Eastern Illinois

8) Who led the Cowboys in rushing touchdowns during the 2010 season?

    A) Marion Barber
    B) Tashard Choice
    C) Jon Kitna
    D) Felix Jones

9) Which former Cowboys great was nicknamed "Manster"?

    A) Harvey Martin
    B) Lee Roy Jordan
    C) Jethro Pugh
    D) Randy White

10) How many seasons did the Cowboys play their home games at Texas Stadium?

    A) 32
    B) 35
    C) 38
    D) 41

11) Who was the most recent Cowboys head coach to win Associated Press (AP) NFL Coach of the Year?

    A) Bill Parcells
    B) Barry Switzer
    C) Tom Landry
    D) Jimmy Johnson

12) Tony Dorsett played his entire NFL career with the Dallas Cowboys.

    A) True
    B) False

13) Where did Cowboys coach Jason Garrett play college football?

    A) Michigan State
    B) North Carolina
    C) Pittsburgh
    D) Princeton

14) Which former Dallas linebacker was known as "Hollywood"?

    A) Lee Roy Jordan
    B) Ken Norton
    C) Thomas Henderson
    D) Chuck Howley

15) Tony Romo won his first-ever game as a starter for the Cowboys.

    A) True
    B) False

16) When was the most recent season Dallas did not play a Monday Night Football game?

    A) 1996
    B) 1999
    C) 2002
    D) 2005

17) The 1967 NFL Championship Game is more commonly known by what name?

    A) Snow Bowl
    B) Ice Bowl
    C) Freezer Bowl
    D) Weather Bowl

18) From which college have the Cowboys drafted the most players?

    A) Alabama
    B) UCLA
    C) Arizona State
    D) Tennessee

19) Who holds Dallas' career rushing yards record?

    A) Emmitt Smith
    B) Walt Garrison
    C) Calvin Hill
    D) Tony Dorsett

20) How many weeks were Cowboys named NFL Rookie of the Week in 2010?

    A) 1
    B) 2
    C) 3
    D) 4

21) Cowboys Stadium has a seating capacity over 100,000.

    A) True
    B) False

22) What year did the Cowboys host their first Thanksgiving Day game?

    A) 1966
    B) 1968
    C) 1970
    D) 1972

23) Which Dallas head coach has the most career wins?

    A) Jimmy Johnson
    B) Barry Switzer
    C) Tom Landry
    D) Chan Gailey

24) What year did Jerry Jones purchase the Dallas Cowboys?

    A) 1986
    B) 1989
    C) 1992
    D) 1995

25) Who holds Dallas' record for passing yards in a single game?

A) Don Meredith
B) Troy Aikman
C) Tony Romo
D) Jon Kitna

26) Which Dallas defender is the Cowboys' career leader in pass interceptions?

A) Deion Sanders
B) Charlie Waters
C) Everson Walls
D) Mel Renfro

27) How many times has Dallas played in the Super Bowl?

A) 6
B) 7
C) 8
D) 9

28) How many touchdown passes did Jon Kitna throw in 2010?

A) 12
B) 14
C) 16
D) 18

29) Have the Cowboys ever played the New York Giants in the postseason?

    A) Yes
    B) No

30) How many times has a Cowboy had greater than 2,000 yards from scrimmage in a single season?

    A) 3
    B) 4
    C) 5
    D) 6

31) Who led the Cowboys in sacks during the 2010 regular season?

    A) Anthony Spencer
    B) DeMarcus Ware
    C) Jay Ratliff
    D) Keith Brooking

32) Which franchise has Dallas played the most in postseason games?

    A) Minnesota Vikings
    B) Green Bay Packers
    C) San Francisco 49ers
    D) St. Louis Rams

33) What are the most regular-season wins the Cowboys have ever had in a single season?

    A) 11
    B) 12
    C) 13
    D) 14

34) Which Cowboy holds the NFL record for consecutive games with a quarterback sack?

    A) DeMarcus Ware
    B) Jim Jeffcoat
    C) Harvey Martin
    D) Charles Haley

35) How many defensive touchdowns did the Cowboys score in 2010?

    A) 3
    B) 4
    C) 5
    D) 6

36) Who is the Cowboys career leader in field goals made?

    A) Nick Folk
    B) Richie Cunningham
    C) Chris Boniol
    D) Rafeal Septien

37) Who is the play-by-play announcer for the Cowboys Radio Network?

   A) Brad Sham
   B) Eric Nadel
   C) Chuck Cooperstein
   D) Verne Lundquist

38) Ed "Too Tall" Jones left the Cowboys in 1979 to pursue what career?

   A) Singing
   B) Wrestling
   C) Boxing
   D) Acting

39) What year did the Dallas Cowboys Cheerleaders make their debut?

   A) 1963
   B) 1966
   C) 1969
   D) 1972

40) What is the name of the Cowboys' official drum line?

   A) Rhythm and Blue
   B) Fantasia
   C) Showband of the Southwest
   D) Dallas Drum

41) The Cowboys traded Herschel Walker to which team?

- A) Green Bay Packers
- B) Cleveland Browns
- C) Philadelphia Eagles
- D) Minnesota Vikings

42) Who holds Dallas' record for receiving yards in a single season?

- A) Drew Pearson
- B) Michael Irvin
- C) Terry Glenn
- D) Terrell Owens

43) Who is the only Cowboy to be named NFL Defensive Player of the Year?

- A) Bob Lilly
- B) Harvey Martin
- C) Everson Walls
- D) Deion Sanders

44) Who is the Cowboys' all-time leader in passing yards?

- A) Troy Aikman
- B) Danny White
- C) Tony Romo
- D) Roger Staubach

45) Which Cowboy holds the team's single-game rushing record?

    A)   Tony Dorsett
    B)   Herschel Walker
    C)   Emmitt Smith
    D)   Julius Jones

46) How many Cowboys have been named Super Bowl MVP?

    A)   5
    B)   6
    C)   7
    D)   8

47) How many one-season head coaches has Dallas had?

    A)   0
    B)   1
    C)   2
    D)   3

48) Did Tom Landry coach another professional football team after leaving the Cowboys?

    A)   Yes
    B)   No

49) Who holds Dallas' record for points scored in a career?

    A) Rafeal Septien
    B) Tony Dorsett
    C) Bob Hayes
    D) Emmitt Smith

50) What season did the Cowboys celebrate their first-ever victory over Green Bay?

    A) 1966
    B) 1970
    C) 1974
    D) 1978

When the city of Dallas was awarded an NFL expansion franchise in January of 1960, owners Clint Murchison Jr. and Bedford Wayne decided to name the team the Dallas Steers. However, there was also a baseball team in the area known as the Dallas Steers. The baseball team was expected to fold before the 1960 season but didn't. As a result, to avoid any confusion, Murchison and Wayne decided to change the name of the football team to the Dallas Cowboys to avoid any confusion.

1) C – 1960 (The Cowboys played their first game on Sept. 24, 1960, a 28-35 loss to the Pittsburgh Steelers.)

2) D – Rowdy (Rowdy has been the official mascot of the Cowboys since 1996.)

3) C – 2009 (Cowboys Stadium, the largest domed stadium in the world, opened in 2009.)

4) A – Ed Jones (Ed "Too Tall" Jones played in 224 career games as a Dallas Cowboy.)

5) B – False (Romo completed 148 of 213 passes [69.5%] while Kitna was 209-318 [65.7%] in 2010.)

6) A – NFC East (The Cowboys play in the NFC East along with the New York Giants, Philadelphia Eagles and Washington Redskins.)

7) D – Eastern Illinois (Romo played college football at Division I-AA Eastern Illinois where he was named Ohio Valley Conference Player of the Year for three consecutive years. In 2002, Romo won the Walter Payton Award, given to the top player in NCAA Division I-AA.)

8) A – Marion Barber (Barber led the Cowboys with four rushing touchdowns in 2010.)

9) D – Randy White (White was described by his opponents as being half man, half monster.)

10) C – 38 (The Cowboys called Texas Stadium home from 1971-08.)

11) D – Jimmy Johnson (Johnson was named AP NFL Coach of the Year following the 1990 season.)

12) B – False (Dorsett played for the Cowboys from 1977-87 before being traded to the Denver Broncos. Dorsett played one season [1988] with the Broncos.)

13) D – Princeton (Garrett began his college career at Princeton, but transferred to Columbia when his father became Columbia's head coach. When Garrett's father resigned following the 1985 season, Jason transferred back to Princeton where he was the starting quarterback in 1987 and 1988.)

14) C – Thomas Henderson (Henderson earned the nickname "Hollywood" for his flashy play and flamboyant lifestyle.)

15) A – True (Romo and the Cowboys beat the Carolina Panthers 35-14 in 2006.)

16) C – 2002 (The Cowboys did not appear in a Monday Night Football game during the 2002 season.)

17) B – Ice Bowl (The game was held in Green Bay with wind chill temperatures of 52 degrees below zero. The Cowboys led the game late in the 4th quarter until Packers quarterback Bart Starr dove into the end zone with just 16 seconds left, giving Green Bay a 21-17 win.)

18) D – Tennessee (The Cowboys have drafted 18 players from the University of Tennessee. The most recent pick was linebacker Kevin Burnett in 2005.)

19) A – Emmitt Smith (Smith rushed for 17,162 yards as a Cowboy.)

20) B – 2 (Dez Bryant [Week 7] and Sean Lee [Week 13])

21) B – False (The seating capacity at Cowboys Stadium is 80,000. The maximum capacity, including standing room, is 110,000.)

22) A – 1966 (The Cowboys hosted their first Thanksgiving Day game in 1966, a 26-14 win over the Cleveland Browns.)

23) C – Tom Landry (Landry won 270 games [including playoffs] from 1960-88.)

24) B – 1989 (Jones purchased the Dallas Cowboys in 1989 for $150 million.)

25) A – Don Meredith (Meredith threw for 460 yards versus the San Francisco 49ers in 1963.)

26) D – Mel Renfro (Renfro recorded 52 career interceptions for the Cowboys.)

27) C – 8 (Super Bowl V, VI, X, XII, XIII, XVII, XVIII and XXX.)

28) C – 16 (Kitna threw 16 touchdown passes and 12 interceptions in 2010.)

29) A – Yes (The Cowboys lost 17-21 to the Giants in the 2007 NFC Divisional game, their only postseason meeting.)

30) A – 3 (Herschel Walker [2,019 in 1988] and Emmitt Smith [2,048 in 1992 and 2,148 in 1995])

31) B – DeMarcus Ware (Ware recorded 15.5 sacks during the 2010 season.)

32) D – St. Louis Rams (The Cowboys have faced the Rams eight times in the postseason, posting a 4-4 record.)

33) C – 13 (The Cowboys won 13 games in 1992 and again in 2007.)

34) A – DeMarcus Ware (Ware shares the NFL record of 10 consecutive games with at least one sack.)

35) B – 4 (The Cowboys returned three interceptions and one fumble for touchdowns in 2010.)

36) D – Rafeal Septien (Septien is the Cowboys' career leader with 162 field goals made.)

37) A – Brad Sham (Sham has been the voice of the Cowboys since 1984.)

38) C – Boxing (After five seasons with the Cowboys, Jones left the team to pursue a heavyweight boxing career. Jones was 6-0 with five knockouts before rejoining the Cowboys in 1980.)

39) D – 1972 (The Dallas Cowboys Cheerleaders made their debut in 1972. Prior to 1972, a group consisting of local high school students known as the CowBelles and Beaux cheered at Cowboy games.)

40) A – Rhythm and Blue (The Rhythm and Blue is made up of a percussion troop and drum line along with a dance team.)

41) D – Minnesota Vikings (In what would become known as "the trade," the Cowboys traded Walker to the Vikings for five players and eight draft picks.)

42) B – Michael Irvin (Irvin had 1,603 receiving yards during the 1995 season.)

43) B – Harvey Martin (Martin was named NFL Defensive Player of the Year in 1977.)

44) A – Troy Aikman (Aikman completed 2,898 passes for 32,942 yards in his Cowboys career.)

45) C – Emmitt Smith (Smith rushed for 237 yards on 30 carries versus the Philadelphia Eagles in 1993.)

46) C – 7 (Chuck Howley [V], Roger Staubach [VI], Randy White and Harvey Martin [XII], Troy Aikman [XXVII], Emmitt Smith [XXVIII] and Larry Brown [XXX])

47) A – 0 (The Cowboys have never had a head coach last just one season.)

48) B – No (Dallas was Landry's first and only head coaching job.)

49) D – Emmitt Smith (Smith is the Cowboys' all-time leading scorer with 986 career points scored.)

50) B – 1970 (The Cowboys beat the Packers 16-3 in 1970.)

Note: All answers valid as of the end of the 2010 season, unless otherwise indicated in the question itself.

1) Who was the first Cowboy to rush for 1,000 yards in a season?

Answers begin on page 37

    A)   Calvin Hill
    B)   Don Perkins
    C)   Tony Dorsett
    D)   Duane Thomas

2) Who is the only Cowboy to wear jersey No. 74?

    A)   Harvey Martin
    B)   Rayfield Wright
    C)   Nate Newton
    D)   Bob Lilly

3) When was the last time the Cowboys drafted a quarterback in the first round?

    A)   1983
    B)   1989
    C)   1995
    D)   2000

4) Which decade did Dallas have the best winning percentage?

    A)   1970s
    B)   1980s
    C)   1990s
    D)   2000s

5) Does Dallas have an all-time winning record against the Philadelphia Eagles during the regular season?

    A) Yes
    B) No

6) What is Dallas' record for most consecutive 10-win seasons?

    A) 5
    B) 7
    C) 9
    D) 11

7) What are the most rushing yards by the Cowboys in a Super Bowl?

    A) 187
    B) 218
    C) 234
    D) 252

8) Where did former Cowboys head coach Chan Gailey play college football?

    A) Florida
    B) USC
    C) Arkansas
    D) Penn State

9) Emmitt Smith became the NFL's all-time leading rusher in a 2002 game versus which opponent?

   A) New Orleans Saints
   B) New York Giants
   C) Minnesota Vikings
   D) Seattle Seahawks

10) Do the Cowboys have a winning record in games following a bye week?

   A) Yes
   B) No

11) What are the most points the Cowboys allowed in a postseason game?

   A) 31
   B) 35
   C) 38
   D) 42

12) How many teams has Dallas played 50 or more times in the regular season?

   A) 4
   B) 5
   C) 6
   D) 7

13) The Cowboys have never lost an NFC Championship Game played in Dallas.

    A) True
    B) False

14) Who was the last player to gain greater than 200 yards rushing against Dallas?

    A) Duce Staley
    B) Charlie Garner
    C) Barry Sanders
    D) Warrick Dunn

15) How many of Jimmy Johnson's assistant coaches became head coaches in the NFL?

    A) 3
    B) 4
    C) 5
    D) 6

16) Which of the following Cowboys never led the NFL in touchdown receptions?

    A) Frank Clarke
    B) Terrell Owens
    C) Michael Irvin
    D) Lance Rentzel

17) Against which team was Dallas' first-ever NFL win?

    A) Philadelphia Eagles
    B) Pittsburgh Steelers
    C) Chicago Bears
    D) Baltimore Colts

18) When was the last time the Cowboys had over 500 yards of total offense in a postseason game?

    A) 1980
    B) 1985
    C) 1991
    D) 1998

19) How many times has Dallas had the No. 1 overall draft pick?

    A) 1
    B) 2
    C) 3
    D) 4

20) Emmitt Smith rushed for more than 1,000 yards as a rookie.

    A) True
    B) False

21) How many yards is the longest rushing play in Dallas history?

    A) 90
    B) 93
    C) 96
    D) 99

22) Which Dallas defender holds the franchise record for career fumble recoveries?

    A) Lee Roy Jordan
    B) Cliff Harris
    C) Dave Edwards
    D) Ed "Too Tall" Jones

23) Who holds the Cowboys' single season record for receptions by a running back?

    A) Ron Springs
    B) Herschel Walker
    C) Richie Anderson
    D) Emmitt Smith

24) How many times has Dallas played in the NFC Wild Card Playoff Game?

    A) 4
    B) 6
    C) 8
    D) 10

25) Dallas holds the NFL record for consecutive winning seasons.

    A) True
    B) False

26) What year did the Cowboys win their first-ever postseason game?

    A) 1963
    B) 1965
    C) 1967
    D) 1969

27) Where did the Cowboys play their home games from 1960-70?

    A) Ownby Stadium
    B) Memorial Stadium
    C) Burnett Field
    D) Cotton Bowl

28) How many Dallas players have been named AP NFL Offensive Rookie of the Year?

    A) 2
    B) 3
    C) 4
    D) 5

29) How many years did Mike Ditka play football for the Cowboys?

    A) 2
    B) 3
    C) 4
    D) 5

30) How many punt return touchdowns did Deion Sanders have as a Cowboy?

    A) 3
    B) 4
    C) 5
    D) 6

31) What is Dallas' all-time longest recorded punt?

    A) 72 yards
    B) 79 yards
    C) 84 yards
    D) 90 yards

32) Do the Cowboys have an all-time winning record against current AFC teams?

    A) Yes
    B) No

33) Who is the only Cowboy to have more than 100 receptions in a single season?

   A) Michael Irvin
   B) Miles Austin
   C) Drew Pearson
   D) Jason Witten

34) Who holds the Dallas record for longest fumble recovery return for a touchdown?

   A) Deion Sanders
   B) Chuck Howley
   C) Michael Downs
   D) Greg Ellis

35) To which team did Dallas suffer the biggest loss in its first NFL season?

   A) Detroit Lions
   B) Cleveland Browns
   C) Green Bay Packers
   D) Baltimore Colts

36) Who was Dallas' first regular season opponent at Cowboys Stadium?

   A) New York Giants
   B) Baltimore Ravens
   C) St. Louis Rams
   D) Tennessee Titans

37) Which Cowboy defender holds the NFL record of nine career postseason interceptions?

    A) Cliff Harris
    B) Everson Walls
    C) Darren Woodson
    D) Charlie Waters

38) Which Cowboy played in the most Pro Bowls?

    A) Emmitt Smith
    B) Bob Lilly
    C) Randy White
    D) Larry Allen

39) Who holds Dallas' record for passing yards in a season?

    A) Troy Aikman
    B) Danny White
    C) Tony Romo
    D) Drew Bledsoe

40) Cowboy receiver Bob Hayes won two Gold Medals at the 1968 Olympics.

    A) True
    B) False

41) Who holds Dallas' record for receiving yards in a postseason game?

    A) Rocket Ismail
    B) Michael Irvin
    C) Bob Hayes
    D) Tony Hill

42) Who holds the Cowboys' record for most touchdown passes in a season?

    A) Troy Aikman
    B) Tony Romo
    C) Don Meredith
    D) Danny White

43) Who holds the Dallas record for longest punt return?

    A) Bryan McCann
    B) Bob Hayes
    C) Deion Sanders
    D) Dennis Morgan

44) How many Dallas players were selected to the 2008 Pro Bowl?

    A) 11
    B) 12
    C) 13
    D) 14

45) Did Roger Staubach have greater than 25,000 career passing yards?

   A) Yes
   B) No

46) Who holds the Cowboys' record for career sacks?

   A) DeMarcus Ware
   B) Harvey Martin
   C) Charles Haley
   D) Jim Jeffcoat

47) How many times has a Cowboy had more than 1,250 yards receiving in a single season?

   A) 6
   B) 8
   C) 10
   D) 12

48) Former Dallas head coach Tom Landry is famous for wearing which article of clothing?

   A) Hawaiian Shirt
   B) Fedora
   C) Bow Tie
   D) Fur Coat

49) In how many decades have the Cowboys won at least 80 games?

    A) 2
    B) 3
    C) 4
    D) 5

50) Who is the most recent Cowboy honored with the Walter Payton Award – NFL Man of The Year?

    A) Troy Aikman
    B) D.D. Lewis
    C) Tony Romo
    D) Emmitt Smith

During the late 1970s, Dallas routinely selected the highest rated player on their draft board regardless of position. However, in the third round of the 1979 NFL Draft the Cowboys bucked this tradition. With the 76th overall pick, the Cowboys selected tight end Doug Cosbie from Santa Clara, even though he was not the highest rated player on their draft board at the time. Cosbie went on to play 10 seasons for the Cowboys, catching 300 passes for 3,728 yards and 30 touchdowns. Cosbie was a three-time Pro Bowler and held several Cowboys tight end receiving records at the time of his retirement, making his mark on the legacy of great tight ends in Cowboys history. So it appears that Dallas made the right decision...or did they? The player rated highest on their draft board in 1979 was none other than Hall of Famer Joe Montana.

1) A – Calvin Hill (Hill rushed for 1,036 yards in 1972.)

2) D – Bob Lilly (Lilly, known as "Mr. Cowboy," was Dallas' first-ever draft pick and wore No. 74 from 1961-74.)

3) B – 1989 (The Cowboys drafted UCLA quarterback Troy Aikman with the No. 1 overall pick in the 1989 NFL Draft.)

4) A – 1970s (The Cowboys were 105-39 during the 1970s, a .729 winning percentage.)

5) A – Yes (The Cowboys are 56-44 all-time versus the Eagles during the regular season, a .560 winning percentage.)

6) B – 7 (The Cowboys won 10 or more games every year from 1975-81.)

7) D – 252 (The Cowboys rushed for 252 yards in a 24-3 victory over the Miami Dolphins in Super Bowl VI.)

8) A – Florida (Gailey was a quarterback and three-year letterman for the Florida Gators from 1971-73.)

9) D – Seattle Seahawks (Smith's 11-yard run in the fourth quarter of a 14-17 loss to the Seahawks pushed him past Walter Payton as the NFL's all-time leading rusher.)

10) A – Yes (The Cowboys are 16-6 all-time following a bye week.)

11) C – 38 (The Cowboys have allowed 38 points in a postseason game three times. The most recent was a 28-38 loss to the San Francisco 49ers in the 1994 NFC Championship Game.)

12) A – 4 (Philadelphia Eagles [100], Washington Redskins [100], New York Giants [97] and Arizona Cardinals [85])

13) B – False (The Cowboys lost 28-38 to the San Francisco 49ers in the 1994 NFC Championship Game in Dallas.)

14) D – Warrick Dunn (Dunn rushed for 210 yards for the Tampa Bay Buccaneers versus the Cowboys Dec. 3, 2000.)

15) B – 4 (Offensive coordinator Norv Turner [Redskins/Raiders], defensive coordinator Dave Wannstedt [Bears/Dolphins], defensive line coach Butch Davis [Browns] and secondary coach Dave Campo [Cowboys])

16) C – Michael Irvin (Clarke led the NFL in touchdown receptions in 1962 [14], Hayes in 1966 [13] and Owens in 2006 [13].)

17) B – Pittsburgh Steelers (The Cowboys beat the Steelers 27-24 on Sept. 17, 1961.)

18) A – 1980 (The Cowboys racked up 528 yards of total offense versus the Los Angeles Rams in the 1980 NFC Wild Card Game.)

19) C – 3 (The Cowboys have had the No. 1 overall draft pick three times: Ed "Too Tall" Jones [1974], Troy Aikman [1989] and Russell Maryland [1991].)

20) B – False (Smith rushed for 937 yards on 241 carries in 1990.)

21) D – 99 (In 1983, Tony Dorsett raced 99 yards for a touchdown versus the Minnesota Vikings on Monday Night Football.)

22) D – Ed "Too Tall" Jones (Jones recovered 19 fumbles during his Cowboys career.)

23) B – Herschel Walker (Walker caught 76 passes for 837 yards in 1986.)

24) D – 10 (The Cowboys are 5-5 all-time when playing in the NFC Wild Card Game.)

25) A – True (The Cowboys hold the NFL record with 20 consecutive winning seasons [1966-85].)

26) C – 1967 (The Cowboys beat the Cleveland Browns 52-14 in 1967.)

27) D – Cotton Bowl (The Cowboys called the Cotton Bowl home from 1960-70.)

28) B – 3 (Calvin Hill [1969], Tony Dorsett [1977], and Emmitt Smith [1990])

29) C – 4 (Ditka played for the Cowboys from 1969-72.)

30) B – 4 (Sanders returned four punts for touchdowns as a Cowboy, a team record.)

31) C – 84 yards (Ron Widby booted an 84-yard punt versus the New Orleans Saints in 1968.)

32) A – Yes (The Cowboys are 94-83 all-time versus the AFC, a .531 winning percentage.)

33) A – Michael Irvin (Irvin had a franchise record 111 receptions in 1995.)

34) D – Greg Ellis (Ellis returned a fumble 98 yards for a touchdown versus the Arizona Cardinals in 1999.)

35) B – Cleveland Browns (The Cowboys lost 7-48 to the Browns in Week 4 of the 1960 season.)

36) A – New York Giants (On Sept. 20, 2009, the Cowboys lost to the Giants 31-33 in front of a record crowd of 105,121.)

37) D – Charlie Waters (In 12 seasons as a Cowboy, Waters intercepted nine postseason passes.)

38) B – Bob Lilly (Lilly played in 11 Pro Bowls [1962, 64-73].)

39) C – Tony Romo (Romo completed 347 of 550 pass attempts for 4,483 yards in 2009.)

40) B – False (Hayes won two Gold Medals in track and field at the 1964 Olympics held in Tokyo, Japan.)

41) B – Michael Irvin (Irvin caught 12 passes for 192 yards versus the San Francisco 49ers in the 1994 playoffs.)

42) B – Tony Romo (Romo threw 36 touchdown passes for the Cowboys in 2007.)

43) D – Dennis Morgan (Morgan returned a punt 98 yards for a touchdown in 1974.)

44) C – 13 (The Cowboys sent a record 13 players to the Pro Bowl, including nine starters.)

45) B – No (Staubach passed for 22,700 yards in his Cowboys career.)

46) D – Jim Jeffcoat (Jeffcoat is the Cowboys' franchise leader with 94.5 career sacks.)

47) A – 6 (The Cowboys have had a player more than 1,250 yards receiving in a season six times. The most recent player to do it was Miles Austin with 1,320 yards in 2009.)

48) B – Fedora (This hat style became a signature piece of Landry's wardrobe during his time on the Dallas sidelines.)

49) B – 3 (1970s, 1990s and 2000s)

50) A – Troy Aikman (Aikman won the award in 1997. The only other Cowboy to win the award was Roger Staubach in 1978.)

Note: All answers valid as of the end of the 2010 season, unless otherwise indicated in the question itself.

1) How many times has Dallas lost in the NFC Championship Game?

Answers begin on page 56

    A) 4
    B) 5
    C) 6
    D) 7

2) What is the Cowboys' all-time winning percentage on Thanksgiving Day?

    A) .505
    B) .588
    C) .640
    D) .703

3) Which year was Dallas' first-ever 10-win season?

    A) 1963
    B) 1966
    C) 1969
    D) 1972

4) Which Cowboys head coach has the second most wins while at Dallas?

    A) Barry Switzer
    B) Bill Parcells
    C) Wade Phillips
    D) Jimmy Johnson

5) What is Dallas' largest margin of victory in a postseason game?

    A) 32
    B) 35
    C) 38
    D) 41

6) Who holds the Cowboys' career record for receiving yards?

    A) Michael Irvin
    B) Drew Pearson
    C) Jay Novacek
    D) Bob Hayes

7) What is the Cowboys team record for most rushing yards in a single game?

    A) 319
    B) 338
    C) 354
    D) 372

8) How many combined kickoffs and punts were returned for touchdowns by the Cowboys in 2010?

    A) 2
    B) 3
    C) 4
    D) 5

9) What is the Dallas record for point after touchdowns made in a single game?

    A) 6
    B) 7
    C) 8
    D) 9

10) Who holds the Dallas record for longest touchdown reception?

    A) Alvin Harper
    B) Tony Dorsett
    C) Jason Tucker
    D) Bob Hayes

11) D.D. Lewis holds the Dallas record for most postseason games as a Cowboy.

    A) True
    B) False

12) How many career 300-yard passing games does Tony Romo have as a Cowboy?

    A) 22
    B) 26
    C) 30
    D) 34

13) What is the Cowboys' record for fewest rushing yards allowed in a single game?

A) 4
B) 7
C) 10
D) 13

14) Which Cowboys defender holds the record for pass interceptions in a single season?

A) Mel Renfro
B) Dennis Thurman
C) Everson Walls
D) Michael Downs

15) Which Cowboys coach has the highest career regular-season winning percentage?

A) Tom Landry
B) Jimmy Johnson
C) Wade Phillips
D) Barry Switzer

16) How many quarterbacks have played 50 or more games with Dallas?

A) 6
B) 7
C) 8
D) 9

17) Who led the Cowboys in total tackles in 2010?

    A) Bradie James
    B) Gerald Sensabaugh
    C) Terence Newman
    D) Keith Brooking

18) What is the Cowboys' record for most consecutive home losses?

    A) 10
    B) 12
    C) 14
    D) 16

19) When was the last time the season-leading passer for Dallas had fewer than 1,500 yards passing?

    A) 1974
    B) 1983
    C) 1992
    D) 2001

20) Who was the most recent receiver to lead the Cowboys in scoring?

    A) Terry Glenn
    B) Bob Hayes
    C) Lance Alworth
    D) Michael Irvin

21) What is Dallas' all-time winning percentage at home (regular season and postseason)?

    A) .478
    B) .562
    C) .653
    D) .721

22) The Cowboys won 10 or more games every year during the 1970s.

    A) True
    B) False

23) Who holds the Cowboys' record for pass receptions in a game?

    A) Lance Rentzel
    B) Michael Irvin
    C) Doug Cosbie
    D) Jason Witten

24) Who is the only Cowboy to win the NFL Comeback Player of the Year Award?

    A) Danny White
    B) Adam Jones
    C) Greg Ellis
    D) Drew Bledsoe

25) Dallas' Tom Landry won more playoff games than any coach in NFL History.

    A) True
    B) False

26) How many overtime games did Dallas play in 2010?

    A) 0
    B) 1
    C) 2
    D) 3

27) What is the Cowboys' franchise record for points scored in a season?

    A) 448
    B) 461
    C) 479
    D) 493

28) What is the Dallas team record for sacks in a season?

    A) 60
    B) 62
    C) 64
    D) 66

29) Which Hall of Fame NBA coach was drafted by the Cowboys?

    A) Phil Jackson
    B) Chuck Daly
    C) Lenny Wilkens
    D) Pat Riley

30) Who was the first Cowboy to be inducted into the Cowboys' Ring of Honor?

    A) Don Perkins
    B) Bob Lilly
    C) Don Meredith
    D) Mel Renfro

31) How many regular-season games did a Cowboys running back rush for 100 yards in 2010?

    A) 2
    B) 4
    C) 6
    D) 8

32) What was the Cowboys' franchise record for consecutive seasons without a postseason appearance?

    A) 4
    B) 5
    C) 6
    D) 7

33) Against which AFC team does Dallas have the highest all-time winning percentage (min. 3 games)?

    A)   San Diego Chargers
    B)   New York Jets
    C)   Cincinnati Bengals
    D)   Indianapolis Colts

34) How did Dallas score its first points in Super Bowl VI?

    A)   Field Goal
    B)   Rushing Touchdown
    C)   Touchdown Pass
    D)   Kickoff Return

35) Has Dallas ever failed to rush for 1,000 yards as a team in a season?

    A)   Yes
    B)   No

36) Who is the only Cowboy to start 200 or more games?

    A)   Nate Newton
    B)   Emmitt Smith
    C)   Ed "Too Tall" Jones
    D)   Tom Rafferty

37) Who was the Cowboys' first round pick in the 2011 NFL Draft?

    A) Bruce Carter
    B) Tyron Smith
    C) David Arkin
    D) DeMarco Murray

38) Who holds the Cowboys' record for quarterback sacks in a single season?

    A) Jim Jeffcoat
    B) Greg Ellis
    C) Too Tall Jones
    D) DeMarcus Ware

39) How many Cowboys Ring of Honor inductees are there?

    A) 15
    B) 17
    C) 19
    D) 21

40) When was the last season the leading rusher for Dallas gained fewer than 500 yards?

    A) 1981
    B) 1985
    C) 1989
    D) 1993

41) When was the last time the Cowboys went undefeated in the preseason?

   A) 2004
   B) 2006
   C) 2008
   D) 2010

42) What is Dallas' all-time record for largest margin of victory?

   A) 38 points
   B) 41 points
   C) 45 points
   D) 49 points

43) When was the last time the Cowboys gave up a safety?

   A) 2004
   B) 2006
   C) 2008
   D) 2010

44) Who is the Cowboys' career leader in yards per punt return average (min. 25 returns)?

   A) Bob Hayes
   B) Deion Sanders
   C) Reggie Swinton
   D) Kelvin Martin

45) Who scored the first touchdown for the Cowboys in the 2009 NFC Wild Card Playoff game versus the Eagles?

    A) Jason Witten
    B) Patrick Crayton
    C) John Phillips
    D) Tashard Choice

46) Did Tom Landry win his final game as the Cowboys head coach?

    A) Yes
    B) No

47) How many interceptions did the Cowboys return for touchdowns in 2010?

    A) 1
    B) 3
    C) 5
    D) 7

48) How many Dallas receivers had 40 or more receptions during the 2010 regular season?

    A) 2
    B) 3
    C) 4
    D) 5

49) When was the most recent season Dallas led the NFC in rushing defense?

A) 1997
B) 2000
C) 2003
D) 2006

50) What is Dallas' record for most consecutive playoff losses?

A) 3
B) 4
C) 5
D) 6

One of the most famous plays in NFL history took place in a 1975 divisional playoff game between the Dallas Cowboys and Minnesota Vikings. The Cowboys trailed the Vikings 14-10 with just 32 seconds left in the game and had possession at midfield. At this point, Quarterback Roger Staubach took the shotgun snap and impulsively heaved a long pass down the right sideline in the direction of wide receiver Drew Pearson. As the Minnesota defender fell down, Pearson caught the ball at the 5-yard line and backed into the end zone giving Dallas the lead. The extra point made the final score 17-14 in favor of Dallas. After the game Staubach, a Catholic, admitted to closing his eyes and saying a Hail Mary prayer while the ball was in the air. His prayer was answered and, to this day, whenever a team attempts a long desperation pass, it is referred to as a "Hail Mary."

Cowboysology Trivia Challenge

1) C – 6 (The Cowboys are 8-6 all-time in NFC Championship Game appearances.)
2) C – .640 (The Cowboys are 27-15-1 all-time on Thanksgiving Day, a .640 winning percentage.)
3) B – 1966 (The Cowboys were 10-3-1 in 1966.)
4) D – Jimmy Johnson (Including the postseason, Johnson won 51 games as Cowboys head coach.)
5) C – 38 (Dallas has beaten their opponent by 38 points twice in franchise history, most recently in 1982 with a 38-0 victory over the Tampa Bay Buccaneers.)
6) A – Michael Irvin (Irvin had 750 receptions for 11,904 yards with the Cowboys.)
7) C – 354 (The Cowboys rushed for 354 yards versus the Baltimore Colts in 1981.)
8) B – 3 (The Cowboys returned three punts for touchdowns in 2010.)
9) C – 8 (Danny Villanueva [1966], Mike Clark [1968] and Rafeal Septien [1980])
10) D – Bob Hayes (Hayes caught a 95-yard touchdown pass from Don Meredith versus the Washington Redskins in 1966.)
11) A – True (Lewis played in a franchise record 27 postseason games for the Cowboys.)
12) B – 26 (Romo has thrown for 300 or more yards 26 times as a Cowboy.)
13) B – 7 (In 1966, the Cowboys allowed just seven rushing yards to the Pittsburgh Steelers in a 52-21 win.)

14) C – Everson Walls (Walls intercepted 11 passes for the Cowboys in 1981.)

15) D – Barry Switzer (Switzer was 40-25 [.625] in five seasons as the Cowboys head coach.)

16) B – 7 (Danny White [166], Troy Aikman [165], Roger Staubach [131], Don Meredith [104], Craig Morton [97], Tony Romo [67] and Eddie LeBaron [52])

17) A – Bradie James (James led the Cowboys with 118 tackles in 2010.)

18) C – 14 (The Cowboys lost 14 consecutive home games from 1988-89, an NFL record they share with the 2008-10 St. Louis Rams.)

19) D – 2001 (Quincy Carter led the Cowboys with 1,072 passing yards in 2001.)

20) B – Bob Hayes (Hayes led the Cowboys with 66 points scored in 1967.)

21) C – .653 (The Cowboys are 267-141-4 all-time at home, a .653 winning percentage.)

22) B – False (The Cowboys won at least 10 games every year except 1974 when they finished 8-6.)

23) D – Jason Witten (Witten caught 15 passes for 138 yards versus the Detroit Lions in 2007.)

24) C – Greg Ellis (Ellis won the award in 2007 after recovering from a torn Achilles suffered during the previous season.)

25) A – True (Landry won 20 career NFL playoff games, one more than the legendary Don Shula.)

26) B – 1 (The Cowboys beat the Indianapolis Colts 38-35 in overtime in Week 13.)

27) C – 479 (The Cowboys scored 479 points in 1983, a 29.9 points-per-game average.)

28) B – 62 (The Cowboys registered 62 team sacks during the 1985 season.)

29) D – Pat Riley (Riley was drafted by the Cowboys in the 11th round of the 1967 NFL Draft as a wide receiver.)

30) B – Bob Lilly (Lilly was inducted into the Cowboys Ring of Honor in 1975.)

31) A – 2 (Felix Jones rushed for 109 yards versus the Tennessee Titans and Tashard Choice rushed for 100 yards versus the Indianapolis Colts.)

32) C – 6 (The Cowboys missed the playoffs in each of their first six seasons in the league [1960-65].)

33) B – New York Jets (The Cowboys are 7-2 all-time versus the Jets, a .778 winning percentage.)

34) A – Field Goal (Mike Clark kicked a 9-yard field goal to give the Cowboys a 3-0 lead over the Miami Dolphins.)

35) B – No (The Cowboys lowest season total came in 1960 when they rushed for 1,049 yards.)

36) C – Ed "Too Tall" Jones (Jones started 203 games in his Cowboys career.)

37) B – Tyron Smith (Smith, an offensive tackle from USC, was the ninth overall pick.)

38) D – DeMarcus Ware (Ware recorded 20 quarterback sacks in 2008.)

39) B – 17 (The Cowboys have inducted 17 members to the Ring of Honor. The most recent inductees were Troy Aikman, Emmitt Smith and Michael Irvin in 2005.)

40) C – 1989 (Paul Palmer led the Cowboys with 446 rushing yards in 1989.)

41) B – 2006 (The Cowboys were 3-0-1 during the 2006 preseason.)

42) D – 49 points (The Cowboys beat the Philadelphia Eagles 56-7 in 1966.)

43) C – 2008 (Tony Romo was sacked in the end zone by New York Giant Mathias Kiwanuka in 2008.)

44) B – Deion Sanders (Sanders returned 89 punts for 1,184 yards, a 13.3 yards per return average.)

45) C – John Phillips (Tony Romo threw a 1-yard touchdown pass to tight end Phillips in the 2nd quarter.)

46) B – No (The Cowboys lost to the Philadelphia Eagles 7-23, finishing the season 3-13 and last in the NFC East.)

47) B – 3 (Sean Lee, Bryan McCann and Orlando Scandrick each returned an interception for a touchdown in 2010.)

48) C – 4 (Jason Witten [94], Miles Austin [69], Felix Jones [48], and Dez Bryant [45])

49) C – 2003 (The Cowboys led the NFC by allowing just 89.1 rushing yards per game in 2003.)

50) D – 6 (The Cowboys lost six consecutive playoff games between 1996 and 2007.)

Note: All answers valid as of the end of the 2010 season, unless otherwise indicated in the question itself.

1) When was the most recent season a Cowboys game resulted in a tie?

Answers begin on page 75

   A) 1962
   B) 1969
   C) 1974
   D) 1980

2) Which opponent handed Dallas its worst defeat in 2010?

   A) New York Giants
   B) Tennessee Titans
   C) Jacksonville Jaguars
   D) Green Bay Packers

3) How many times have the Cowboys led the league in points scored?

   A) 3
   B) 4
   C) 5
   D) 6

4) The Cowboys led the league in rush defense each year from 1966-69.

   A) True
   B) False

5) Which player holds Dallas' record for most field goals made in a season?

    A) Richie Cunningham
    B) Nick Folk
    C) Chris Boniol
    D) Eddie Murray

6) Who was the most recent head coach to lose his first regular-season game with Dallas?

    A) Wade Phillips
    B) Dave Campo
    C) Chan Gailey
    D) Bill Parcells

7) What is Dallas' record for most consecutive years appearing in the postseason?

    A) 7
    B) 8
    C) 9
    D) 10

8) How many Dallas head coaches are in the Pro Football Hall of Fame?

    A) 1
    B) 2
    C) 3
    D) 4

9) Which AFC team has Dallas never beaten?

    A)   Jacksonville Jaguars
    B)   Oakland Raiders
    C)   Houston Texans
    D)   Baltimore Ravens

10) Barry Switzer won an NCAA National Championship at Miami prior to coaching the Dallas Cowboys.

    A)   True
    B)   False

11) Which of the following Dallas players was not named AP First-Team All-Pro in 1995?

    A)   Deion Sanders
    B)   Darren Woodson
    C)   Nate Newton
    D)   Emmitt Smith

12) When was the last season a Cowboys defender had three interceptions in the same game?

    A)   1995
    B)   1999
    C)   2003
    D)   2007

13) Which team handed Dallas their all-time worst defeat?

   A) Chicago Bears
   B) New York Giants
   C) Green Bay Packers
   D) Pittsburgh Steelers

14) Who holds Dallas' single-season rushing yards record?

   A) Herschel Walker
   B) Emmitt Smith
   C) Tony Dorsett
   D) Calvin Hill

15) When was the last time the Cowboys were shut out?

   A) 2001
   B) 2003
   C) 2005
   D) 2007

16) Tony Dorsett rushed for greater than 1,000 yards as a rookie.

   A) True
   B) False

17) When is the last time the Cowboys led the NFL in sacks?

   A) 2004
   B) 2006
   C) 2008
   D) 2010

18) How many consecutive seasons did the Cowboys' Michael Irvin have greater than 1,000 yards receiving?

   A) 4
   B) 5
   C) 6
   D) 7

19) What is the Cowboys' record for rushing touchdowns in a game by a single player?

   A) 4
   B) 5
   C) 6
   D) 7

20) Which Dallas quarterback holds the team record for highest passer rating in a single season?

   A) Tony Romo
   B) Troy Aikman
   C) Danny White
   D) Roger Staubach

21) How many total head coaches have the Cowboys had in their history?

    A) 7
    B) 8
    C) 9
    D) 10

22) What is Dallas' largest margin of victory over the Giants?

    A) 31 points
    B) 35 points
    C) 41 points
    D) 45 points

23) Which Cowboys head coach has the second highest winning percentage at Dallas (min. 3 seasons)?

    A) Chan Gailey
    B) Bill Parcells
    C) Tom Landry
    D) Jimmy Johnson

24) Has Dallas played every NFL team at least once?

    A) Yes
    B) No

25) Which Cowboy won the Ed Block Courage Award in 2010?

    A) Jon Kitna
    B) Felix Jones
    C) Sam Hurd
    D) Jason Witten

26) Dallas has an all-time winning record against every NFC East opponent.

    A) True
    B) False

27) Which Dallas quarterback threw the most career interceptions?

    A) Danny White
    B) Roger Staubach
    C) Troy Aikman
    D) Don Meredith

28) Who is the Cowboys' career leader in yards per kickoff return (min. 25 returns)?

    A) Bob Hayes
    B) Herschel Walker
    C) Kevin Williams
    D) Mel Renfro

29) Which decade did Dallas have its lowest winning percentage?

A) 1960s
B) 1980s
C) 1990s
D) 2000s

30) The Cowboys were penalized for greater than 1,000 yards in 2010.

A) True
B) False

31) How many times have the Cowboys played the San Francisco 49ers in the postseason?

A) 5
B) 7
C) 9
D) 11

32) What year did Dallas set an NFL record by allowing just two rushing touchdowns all season?

A) 1968
B) 1977
C) 1985
D) 1995

33) When was the last season the Cowboys recorded a safety?

    A) 2004
    B) 2006
    C) 2008
    D) 2010

34) Which team handed Dallas its worst postseason defeat?

    A) Minnesota Vikings
    B) Los Angeles Rams
    C) San Francisco 49ers
    D) Detroit Lions

35) What is Dallas' record for consecutive regular-season wins?

    A) 6
    B) 8
    C) 10
    D) 12

36) Has Dallas ever led the league in scoring defense?

    A) Yes
    B) No

37) What is the Cowboys' franchise record for fewest points allowed in a 16-game season?

    A) 229
    B) 243
    C) 261
    D) 277

38) When was the last season the Cowboys allowed a two-point conversion?

    A) 2007
    B) 2008
    C) 2009
    D) 2010

39) How many times did Danny White throw four or more touchdown passes in a game?

    A) 4
    B) 6
    C) 8
    D) 10

40) Has Dallas ever hosted the NFL Pro Bowl?

    A) Yes
    B) No

41) Which season did Dallas average a franchise low 12.8 points scored per game?

A) 1960
B) 1973
C) 1989
D) 1997

42) What is the Cowboys' team record for rushing yards in a season?

A) 2,464
B) 2,599
C) 2,678
D) 2,783

43) Which of the following Cowboy quarterbacks never had a 400-yard passing game?

A) Tony Romo
B) Don Meredith
C) Roger Staubach
D) Troy Aikman

44) Who holds the Cowboys' franchise record for career touchdown receptions?

A) Tony Hill
B) Drew Pearson
C) Michael Irvin
D) Bob Hayes

45) Who was the most recent opponent shut out by Dallas?

    A) Houston Texans
    B) Philadelphia Eagles
    C) Tampa Bay Buccaneers
    D) Seattle Seahawks

46) Who holds Dallas' record for most points scored in a single season?

    A) Emmitt Smith
    B) Nick Folk
    C) Richie Cunningham
    D) Rafael Septien

47) What is the Dallas franchise record for total offense in a game?

    A) 603 yards
    B) 628 yards
    C) 652 yards
    D) 679 yards

48) How many members of the NFL's 75th Anniversary All-Time Team played for the Cowboys?

    A) 2
    B) 3
    C) 4
    D) 5

49) Who holds Dallas' career postseason rushing yards record?

    A) Tony Dorsett
    B) Calvin Hill
    C) Emmitt Smith
    D) Robert Newhouse

50) Against which NFL Division does Dallas have the highest all-time winning percentage?

    A) NFC South
    B) AFC East
    C) AFC South
    D) NFC West

Not only was Tom Landry one of the most important figures in the rise of the Dallas Cowboys franchise, but he was also a key innovator in the way the game is still played today. As the New York Giants defensive coordinator in the late 1950s, Landry created the 4-3 defense, a scheme that most NFL teams still employ to this day. As the Dallas Cowboys head coach, Landry created the shot-gun formation and was the first to employ multiple shifts in the offensive formation to confuse defenses. Landry was also the first coach to sign a world-class sprinter to play wide receiver, which in turn led to the creation of the "zone" pass defense. Though the stoic man in the suit and trademark fedora passed away in 2000, his contributions to the NFL will live on forever.

1) B – 1969 (The Cowboys and San Francisco 49ers battled to a 24-24 tie in 1969.)
2) D – Green Bay Packers (The Cowboys lost 7-45 to the Packers in Week 9.)
3) C – 5 (1966, 1968, 1971, 1978 and 1980)
4) A – True (The Cowboys led the league in rush defense four consecutive years [1966-69], an NFL record.)
5) A – Richie Cunningham (Cunningham converted 34 of 37 field goal attempts in 1997.)
6) D – Bill Parcells (The Cowboys lost 13-27 to the Atlanta Falcons in the 2003 season opener.)
7) C – 9 (The Cowboys made the playoffs each year from 1975-83.)
8) A – 1 (Tom Landry)
9) D – Baltimore Ravens (The Cowboys are 0-3 all-time versus the Ravens.)
10) B – False (Switzer won three NCAA National Championships at Oklahoma. Jimmy Johnson won a National Championship at Miami.)
11) A – Deion Sanders (Woodson, Newton and Smith were all named First-Team All-Pro in 1995.)
12) C – 2003 (Terence Newman intercepted three passes versus the Washington Redskins in 2003.)

13) A – Chicago Bears (The Cowboys were defeated 0-44 by the Bears in 1985.)

14) B – Emmitt Smith (Smith rushed for 1,773 yards in 1995.)

15) B – 2003 (The Cowboys lost to the New England Patriots 0-12 in Week 11.)

16) A – True (Despite starting just four games, Dorsett rushed for 1,007 yards as a rookie in 1977.)

17) C – 2008 (The Cowboys led the NFL with 59 quarterback sacks in 2008.)

18) B – 5 (Irvin had over 1,000 yards receiving every year from 1991-95.)

19) A – 4 (The record is shared by Calvin Hill and Emmitt Smith [twice].)

20) D – Roger Staubach (Staubach set the franchise record with a 104.8 quarterback rating in 1971.)

21) B – 8 (In 2010, Jason Garrett became the eighth head coach in Cowboys history.)

22) D – 45 points (The Cowboys beat the Giants 52-7 in 1966.)

23) C – Tom Landry (Landry was 250-162-6 as the Cowboys head coach, a .607 winning percentage.)

24) A – Yes

25) C – Sam Hurd (The Ed Block Courage Award is given each year to one player from each team who is voted by their teammates as a model of inspiration, sportsmanship and courage.)

26) A – True (The Cowboys have an all-time winning record versus the Eagles [56-44], Giants [56-39-2] and Redskins [60-38-2].)

27) C – Troy Aikman (Aikman threw 141 interceptions during his Cowboys career.)

28) D – Mel Renfro (Renfro returned 85 kickoffs for 2,246 yards, a 26.4 yards per return average.)

29) A – 1960s (The Cowboys were 67-65-5 during the 1960s, a .507 winning percentage.)

30) B – False (The Cowboys were penalized 109 times for 863 yards in 2010.)

31) B – 7 (The Cowboys are 5-2 versus the 49ers in postseason play.)

32) A – 1968

33) C – 2008 (The Cowboys Carlos Polk blocked a San Francisco 49ers punt for a safety in 2008.)

34) D – Detroit Lions (The Cowboys lost to the Lions 6-38 in the 1991 Playoffs.)

35) B – 8 (The Cowboys won eight straight games in 1977.)

36) B – No (The Cowboys have never led the league in scoring defense but have ranked second four times.)

37) B – 243 (The Cowboys allowed just 243 points in 1993, a 15.2 points-per-game average.)

38) D – 2010 (The Redskins converted a pair of two-point conversions in a 33-30 Dallas win in 2010.)

39) C – 8 (White threw four or more touchdown passes in a game eight times, a Cowboys record.)

40) A – Yes (The Pro Bowl was played at Dallas' Texas Stadium following the 1972 season.)

41) C – 1989 (The Cowboys scored just 204 points during the 1989 season.)

42) D – 2,783 (The Cowboys rushed for 2,783 yards in 1978.)

43) C – Roger Staubach (Meredith threw for 400+ yards twice, Aikman and Romo once each.)

44) D – Bob Hayes (Hayes caught 71 touchdown passes during his Cowboy career.)

45) B – Philadelphia Eagles (The Cowboys beat the Eagles 24-0 in the 2009 regular season finale.)

46) A – Emmitt Smith (Smith set the franchise record by scoring 150 points in 1995.)

47) C – 652 yards (The Cowboys posted 652 yards of total offense versus the Philadelphia Eagles in 1966.)

48) B – 3 (Bob Lilly [1961-74], Mike Ditka [1969-72] and Lance Alworth [1971-72])

49) C – Emmitt Smith (Smith rushed for 1,586 postseason yards.)

50) A – NFC South (The Cowboys are 46-21 all-time versus the current NFC South teams, a .687 winning percentage.)

Note: All answers valid as of the end of the 2010 season, unless otherwise indicated in the question itself.

1) How many career touchdown passes did Danny White throw for the Cowboys?

Answers begin on page 83

    A) 155
    B) 170
    C) 185
    D) 200

2) What is the Cowboys' longest winning streak in the Dallas-Washington series?

    A) 7
    B) 8
    C) 9
    D) 10

3) How many Cowboys have played in five or more Pro Bowls?

    A) 18
    B) 20
    C) 22
    D) 24

4) Dallas has the most postseason wins in NFL History.

    A) True
    B) False

5) How many rushing touchdowns did Roger Staubach score during his Dallas career?

    A) 16
    B) 20
    C) 24
    D) 28

6) How many times has Dallas played in the NFL Hall of Fame Game Series?

    A) 2
    B) 3
    C) 4
    D) 5

7) What year did the Cowboys finish the season with only one win?

    A) 1961
    B) 1982
    C) 1989
    D) 2000

8) How many Cowboys have been named Pro Bowl MVP?

    A) 3
    B) 4
    C) 5
    D) 6

9) How many different Cowboys have scored a touchdown in the Super Bowl?

   A) 15
   B) 16
   C) 17
   D) 18

10) What are the most points ever scored by Dallas in a single game?

   A) 55
   B) 59
   C) 63
   D) 67

1) A – 155 (White threw 155 career touchdown passes.)
2) C – 9 (The Cowboys won nine consecutive games from 1998-02.)
3) D – 24 (The Cowboys have had 24 players play in five or more Pro Bowls.)
4) A – True (The Cowboys have 33 postseason wins, an NFL record they share with the Pittsburgh Steelers.)
5) B – 20 (Staubach scored 20 career rushing touchdowns.)
6) C – 4 (The Cowboys are 1-3, with their lone win coming in 2010.)
7) C – 1989 (The Cowboys were just 1-15 in 1989.)
8) A – 3 (George Andrie [1969], Mel Renfro [1970] and Michael Irvin [1991])
9) D – 18
10) B – 59 (The Cowboys scored 59 points versus Detroit in 1968 and versus San Francisco in 1980.)

Note: All answers valid as of the end of the 2010 season, unless otherwise indicated in the question itself.

Player / Team Score Sheet

Name:_____

First Quarter			Second Quarter			Third Quarter			Fourth Quarter			Overtime Bonus	
1	16	26	1		26	1		26	1		26	1	
2		27	2		27	2		27	2		27	2	
3		28	3		28	3		28	3		28	3	
4		29	4		29	4		29	4		29	4	
5		30	5		30	5		30	5		30	5	
6		31	6		31	6		31	6		31	6	
7		32	7		32	7		32	7		32	7	
8		33	8		33	8		33	8		33	8	
9		34	9		34	9		34	9		34	9	
10		35	10		35	10		35	10		35	10	
11		36	11		36	11		36	11		36		
12		37	12		37	12		37	12		37		
13		38	13		38	13		38	13		38		
14		39	14		39	14		39	14		39		
15		40	15		40	15		40	15		40		
16		41	16		41	16		41	16		41		
17		42	17		42	17		42	17		42		
18		43	18		43	18		43	18		43		
19		44	19		44	19		44	19		44		
20		45	20		45	20		45	20		45		
21		46	21		46	21		46	21		46		
22		47	22		47	22		47	22		47		
23		48	23		48	23		48	23		48		
24		49	24		49	24		49	24		49		
25		50	25		50	25		50	25		50		

___ x 1 =___   ___ x 2 =___   ___ x 3 =___   ___ x 4 =___   ___ x 4 =___

Multiply total number correct by point value/quarter to calculate totals for each quarter.

Add total of all quarters below.

Total Points:_____

Thank you for playing *Cowboysology Trivia Challenge*.

Additional score sheets are available at:
www.TriviaGameBooks.com

Player / Team Score Sheet

Name:_____

First Quarter			Second Quarter			Third Quarter			Fourth Quarter			Overtime Bonus	
1	C	26	1		26	1		26	1		26	1	
2	D	27	2		27	2		27	2		27	2	
3	A	28	3		28	3		28	3		28	3	
4	A	29	4		29	4		29	4		29	4	
5	B	30	5		30	5		30	5		30	5	
6	A	31	6		31	6		31	6		31	6	
7	D	32	7		32	7		32	7		32	7	
8	A	33	8		33	8		33	8		33	8	
9	D	34	9		34	9		34	9		34	9	
10	C	35	10		35	10		35	10		35	10	
11	D	36	11		36	11		36	11		36		
12	B	37	12		37	12		37	12		37		
13	D	38	13		38	13		38	13		38		
14	C	39	14		39	14		39	14		39		
15	B	40	15		40	15		40	15		40		
16	C	41	16		41	16		41	16		41		
17	B	42	17		42	17		42	17		42		
18	A	43	18		43	18		43	18		43		
19	A	44	19		44	19		44	19		44		
20	C	45	20		45	20		45	20		45		
21	A	46	21		46	21		46	21		46		
22	B	47	22		47	22		47	22		47		
23	C	48	23		48	23		48	23		48		
24	A	49	24		49	24		49	24		49		
25	A	50	25		50	25		50	25		50		

____ x 1 = ____   ____ x 2 = ____   ____ x 3 = ____   ____ x 4 = ____   ____ x 4 = ____

Multiply total number correct by point value/quarter to calculate totals for each quarter.

Add total of all quarters below.

Total Points:_____

Thank you for playing *Cowboysology Trivia Challenge*.

Additional score sheets are available at:
www.TriviaGameBooks.com